NINJA DUAL ZONE AIR FRYER COOKBOOK

EASY & DELICIOUS NINJA FOODI DUAL ZONE AIR FRYER AF300UK RECIPES USING METRIC MEASUREMENT

PHOEBE HOWELLS

© Copyright 2021 - All rights reserved.
ISBN: 9798491232024

The contents of this book may not be reproduced, duplicated or transmitted without direct
written permission from the author.
Under no circumstances will any legal responsibility or blame be held against the publisher for
any reparation, damages, or monetary loss due to the information herein, either directly or
indirectly.

Legal Notice:
This book is copyright protected. This is only for personal use. You cannot amend, distribute,
sell, use, quote or paraphrase any part of the content within this book without the consent of the
author.

Disclaimer Notice:
Please note the information contained within this document is for educational and
entertainment purposes only. Every attempt has been made to provide accurate, up to date and
reliable information. No warranties of any kind are expressed or implied. Readers acknowledge
that the author is not engaging in the rendering of legal, financial, medical or professional
advice. The content of this book has been derived from various sources. Please consult a licensed
professional before attempting any techniques outlined in this book.
By reading this document, the reader agrees that under no circumstances are is the author
responsible for any losses, direct or indirect, which are incurred as a result of the use of
information contained within this document, including, but not limited to, — errors, omissions,
or inaccuracies.

NINJA DUAL ZONE AIR FRYER COOKBOOK | PHOEBE HOWELLS

TABLE OF CONTENT

INTRODUCTION 6

ESSENTIALS OF NINJA FOODI DUAL ZONE AIR FRYER.....................7

BREAKFAST RECIPES 10
EGG AND BACON MUFFINS 11
BREAKFAST ONION OMELET 12
MUSHROOM AND SQUASH TOAST 13
EGG SALAD SANDWICHES 14
DELICIOUS PUMPKIN BREAD................ 15

FISH AND SEAFOOD 16
SALMON CAKES........................... 17
SWAI FISH................................ 18
COCONUT SHRIMP WITH DIPPING SAUCE 19
JUMBO SHRIMP 20
PRAWNS................................. 21
MUSSELS................................22
COD NUGGETS..........................23
BLACK COD WITH BLACK BEAN SAUCE 24
TUNA STEAKS 25
CAJUN SEASONED FRIED CATFISH 26

BEEF, LAMB AND PORK 28
PORK LETTUCE WRAPS 29
BEEF MEATLOAF 30
PORK CHOP BITES WITH MUSHROOMS 31
STUFFED ZUCCHINI BOATS WITH SAUSAGE....32
BROWN SUGAR AND HONEY GLAZED HAM 33
PORK CHOPS PARMIGIANA 34
ROAST LAMB 35
GREEK LAMB BURGERS 36

LAMB MEATBALLS 37
PORK SCHNITZEL.......................38
BEEF AND BROCCOLI 39
STEAK BITES WITH GARLIC BUTTER 40
STEAK BITES WITH MUSHROOMS............ 41
BEEF ROAST AND POTATO FRIES 42
BURGERS 43
TAQUITOS WITH GREEN BEANS................44
BEEF WITH RATATOUILLE 45
GARLIC LAMB CHOPS POTATO WEDGES.......46
LAMB SHANKS SQUASH FRIES 47
TONKATSU WITH WHITE RICE 48
BBQ PORK TENDERLOIN WITH MUSHROOMS...49
PORK LOIN SANDWICH TOMATOES..........50
PORK SCHNITZEL AND POTATO HAY.......... 51

POULTRY 52
YUMMY CHICKEN CUTLETS 53
POPCORN CHICKEN......................54
CHICKEN LEG QUARTERS 55
CHICKEN BURGER 56
BARBEQUE CHICKEN SAUSAGE PIZZA........57
BUFFALO CHICKEN CALZONES 58
DELICIOUS CHICKEN MEATBALLS..............59
PISTACHIO CRUSTED CHICKEN 60
CHICKEN STREET TACOS 61
CHICKEN ENCHILADAS 62

VEGETABLES 64
CRUNCHY VEGGIE CHIPS..................65
PARMESAN DILL FRIED PICKLE CHIPS..........66
CARROT FRIES 67

BUFFALO CAULIFLOWER TOTS	68
BEET CHIPS	69
SPECIAL AVOCADO FRIES	70
FRIED MUSHROOMS	71
COURGETTE FRITTERS	72
TASTY VEGGIE QUESADILLAS	73
KALE CHIPS	74

SNACKS AND DESSERTS **76**
CHOCOLAT E CHIP COOKIES	77
BLUEBERRY MUFFINS	78
PECAN PIE	79
RED VELVET CAKE MIX COOKIES	80
CHERRY PIE BOMBS	81

CONCLUSION **82**
INDEX **83**
MEAL PLAN **85**

INTRODUCTION

The Ninja foodi 2-baskets air fryer has unique dual-zone technology that lets you cook two different meals or bulk of food simultaneously with two different temperatures and cooking time. It is different from the traditional air fryer that has a single basket. It is targeted at busy people who have no time to cook delicious and healthy meals for their families. I recommend this kitchen appliance for your busy life. It is perfect for you and your family.

If you are a housewife, then this ninja foodi 2-baskets air fryer kitchen appliance is an excellent appliance to fulfill all the cooking needed. There are six cooking functions in this appliance. For example, air broil, air fry, bake, reheat, roast, and dehydrate. Take advantage of the recipes provided in this cookbook and enjoy a meal with your family and friends. You can prepare food using your favorite function. Both baskets are non-sticks and easily washable. The useable appliance is especially for those people who love to bake and cook delicious food.

Take advantage of this appliance:
- It saves your time plus energy.
- You can prepare the meal in less time. You didn't need to stand in your kitchen for a long time.
- You can choose your favorite or, according to recipe instruction, cooking function.
- You can use this appliance easily without hesitation.
- You can prepare two different meals in the same setting or different settings.
- Easy to wash this appliance.
- You can prepare bulky food or less if desired.

My cookbook "Ninja foodi 2-baskets air fryer with dual-zone technology" has fifty wholesome recipes. I divided recipes into different chapters such as Breakfast, Dessert, Chicken and poultry recipes, beef, lamb, and pork recipes, Seafood and fish recipes, and vegetable recipes. You can choose from breakfast to dinner recipes from my cookbook and prepare yummy food using Ninja 2 baskets air fryer appliance. Let feed your family and kids healthy and delicious food!
GOOD LUCK!

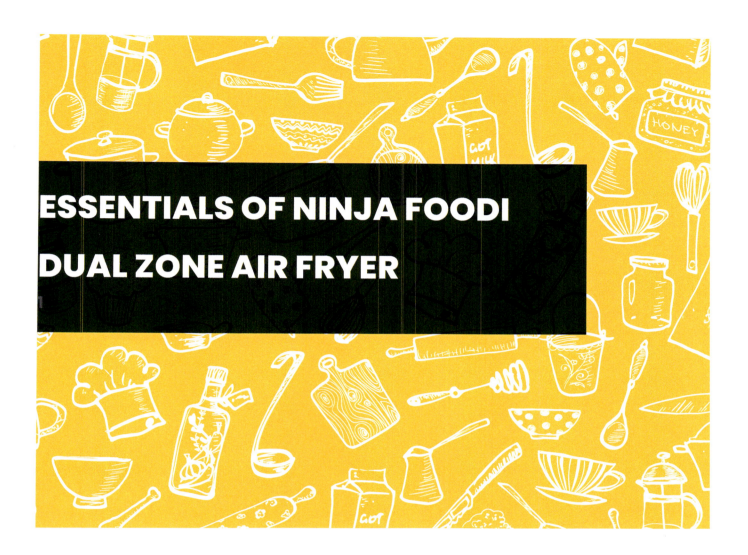

ESSENTIALS OF NINJA FOODI DUAL ZONE AIR FRYER

1. The functions of Ninja Foodi 2-Basket Air Fryer

The ninja foodi 2 baskets air fryer has six cooking functions. If you have this appliance in your kitchen or want to buy it, you should know about it. This Ninja foodi air fryer makes crispy and wholesome food for you and your beloved one. This unique cooking appliance comes with two air fryer baskets. These are marked as "1" and "2". You can open them without click any button. You can remove them by pulling them out. Moreover, it has dual-zone technology.

Air fryer: Air fryer is a standard mode. I added many air fryer recipes in my cookbook. You can choose a recipe and cook food without using little or no oil. It is a beneficial cooking mode.

Bake: Kids love baking food. I added baking recipes also in my book. Press the "bake" option and bake for your kids.

Reheat: Reheat is a vital cooking function. It reheats your leftover food. Simply press the "reheat" button.

Roast: This function turns your appliance into an oven and gives you tender and delicious meat.

Air broil: This cooking function will give you

crispy food. Prepare food for dinner or lunch!

Dehydrate: This mode dehydrates meats, vegetables, and fruits. You can cook food overnight with this option, and your food is ready in the morning.

Temperature mode: You can adjust the temperature according to recipe instructions. If you want to cook two different meals, then adjust two different temperatures.

Time mode: You can adjust cooking time according to recipe cooking instructions.

Finish button: When cooking is done, you can press it, allowing the appliance to turn off both cooking zones.

Match cook mode: This button will automatically allow the appliance to match Zone 2 with Zone 1. It is a beneficial function because you can cook a large amount of food.

Start or pause button: The start/pause button will allow you to stop, initiate, and resume cooking meals.

Power button: The power button is pressed to turn the appliance on and off when needed.

Hold mode: It will appear on the display screen when you press the finish button. When the cooking time of zone 1 is great than zone 2, the hold button will appear for the zone with cooking time, and it will wait for the cooking of another zone to be complete.

2. How to use Ninja foodi 2-basket air fryer

Cooking food with Ninja foodi 2-baskets is very simple. Follow these simple steps to understand how to use this appliance.

Step: 1

Combine all ingredients and prepare meatballs, rolls, patties, or any other meal and divide it into two baskets if food is present in the large amount.

Step: 2

Return basket into Ninja foodi 2-baskets air fryer.

Step: 3

After that, select a method such as "air fryer" or "bake" mode for Zone 1 with "recipe calls" temperature and "recipe calls" cooking time.

Step: 4

Press the "MATCH COOK" button to copy the setting for Zone 2.

Step: 5

Press the "START/PAUSE" button to initiate the cooking.

Step: 6

If you want to flip the food, open the lid, flip over the food, and cook according to recipe cooking time.

Step: 7

When done, remove it from the appliance and transfer it to the serving plate.

Serve food!

3. Maintain and cleaning the appliance

Maintain and clean up Ninja foodi 2 baskets air fryer is quite easy.

- Unplug the appliance before start cleaning. Let cool the appliance if it is hot. Then, start cleaning.

- Remove both air fryer baskets from the appliance. Set aside.

- When cooled, remove the plates and wash them thoroughly.

- Use soapy water and wash the air fryer baskets. But keep in mind; avoid using hard scrubber because it will damage the surface.

- Use soft scrub to clean the food stuck.

- Clean the main unit with a soft piece of cloth.

- When everything has been cleaned, let them dry. Then, return both baskets to the Ninja foodi air fryer.

BREAKFAST RECIPES

EGG AND BACON MUFFINS

 **PREPARATION TIME** 5 MINUTES

 **COOKING TIME** 15 MINUTES

 SERVINGS 1 PERSONS

INGREDIENTS:

- Egg, 2
- Ground pepper and salt, to taste
- Green pesto, 14ml
- Cheddar cheese, 85g, shredded
- Cooked bacon, 142g
- Onion, 1, chopped

PREPARATIONS:

1. Add pesto, salt, pepper, and eggs into the bowl and beat it well.
2. Then, add cheese and combine it well.
3. Pour eggs into the cupcakes tin and top with onion and cooked bacon.
4. Place cupcake tins into the basket. If you want, divide cupcakes into two baskets.
5. Place air fryer basket to the Ninja foodi air fryer.
6. Select the "bake" mode for Zone 1 with 177 degrees C temperature and 15 minutes of cooking time.
7. Press the "MATCH COOK" button to copy the setting for Zone 2.
8. Initiate cooking by pressing the "START/PAUSE" button.
9. When done, serve and enjoy!

Nutrition:

CALORIES: 134KCAL | FAT: 9.7G | CARBOHYDRATE: 1.4G | SUGARS: 21G | FIBER: 0.2G | PROTEIN: 10.1G

BREAKFAST ONION OMELET

 **PREPARATION TIME** 10 MINUTES
 COOKING TIME 12 MINUTES
 SERVINGS 2 PERSONS

INGREDIENTS:

- Eggs, 3
- Pepper and salt, to taste
- Soy sauce, 2ml
- Onion, 1, chopped
- Cheddar cheese, 28g, shredded

PREPARATIONS:

1. Whisk the soy sauce, pepper, salt, and eggs into the bowl.
2. Place chopped onion over the mixture.
3. Place onion mixture into the basket. If you want, divide the onion mixture into two baskets.
4. Place air fryer basket to the Ninja foodi air fryer.
5. Select the "air fry" mode for Zone 1 with 179 degrees C temperature and 12 minutes of cooking time.
6. Press the "MATCH COOK" button to copy the setting for Zone 2.
7. Initiate cooking by pressing the "START/PAUSE" button.
8. When done, remove and serve!

Nutrition:

CALORIES: 115.6KCAL | FAT: 9G | CARBOHYDRATE: 0.7G | SUGARS: 0.3G | FIBER: 0G | PROTEIN: 7.5G

MUSHROOM AND SQUASH TOAST

 **PREPARATION TIME** 10 MINUTES

 **COOKING TIME** 12 MINUTES

 SERVINGS 2 PERSONS

INGREDIENTS:

- Olive oil, 14ml
- Red bell pepper, 1, cut into strips
- Green onions, 2, sliced
- Button or cremini mushrooms, 128g
- Yellow squash, 1, sliced
- Butter, 29ml, softened
- Bread, 4 slices
- Cheese, 64g, soft

PREPARATIONS:

1. Divide vegetables into two baskets.
2. Place air fryer basket to the Ninja foodi air fryer.
3. Select the "air fry" mode for Zone 1 with 177 degrees C temperature and 7 minutes of cooking time.
4. Press the "MATCH COOK" button to copy the setting for Zone 2.
5. Initiate cooking by pressing the "START/PAUSE" button.
6. When done, remove vegetables from the Ninja foodi air fryer.
7. After that, spread butter onto the slices of bread and transfer it to the basket. Adjust the time for three minutes.
8. When done, remove toast from the Ninja foodi air fryer.
9. Place cooked vegetables and cheese onto the toast.
10. Serve and enjoy!

Nutrition:

CALORIES: 249KCAL | FAT: 7.2G | CARBOHYDRATE: 27.2G | SALT: 0.6G | FIBER: 3.1G | PROTEIN: 17.1G

EGG SALAD SANDWICHES

 **PREPARATION TIME** 5 MINUTES

 **COOKING TIME** 15 MINUTES

 SERVINGS 4 PERSONS

INGREDIENTS:
- Eggs, 8
- Mayonnaise, 118ml
- Mustard, 5g
- Salt, 2 ½ g

PREPARATIONS:
1. Divide eggs into two baskets.
2. Place air fryer basket to the Ninja foodi air fryer.
3. Select the "air fry" mode for Zone 1 with 148 degrees C temperature and 15 minutes of cooking time.
4. Press the "MATCH COOK" button to copy the setting for Zone 2.
5. Initiate cooking by pressing the "START/PAUSE" button.
6. When done, remove eggs from the Ninja foodi air fryer.
7. When eggs are cooked, place them into the bowl of ice water.
8. Let cool it for five minutes.
9. When cooled, peel and chop them.
10. Place them into the mixing bowl. Then, add salt, mustard, and mayonnaise and mix it well.
11. Serve egg salad on lettuce wraps or bread.

Nutrition:
CALORIES: 317KCAL | FAT: 29G | CARBOHYDRATE: 1G | SUGAR: 1G | FIBER: 1G | PROTEIN: 17.1G

DELICIOUS PUMPKIN BREAD

 **PREPARATION TIME** 10 MINUTES

 **COOKING TIME** 45 MINUTES

 SERVINGS 16 PERSONS

INGREDIENTS:

- Pumpkin, 425g, pureed
- Eggs, 3
- Vegetable oil, 236ml
- Sugar, 320g
- Flour, 384g
- Bicarb soda, 10g
- Salt, 5g
- Cinnamon, 5g
- Chocolate chips or cranberries, 64g, optional

PREPARATIONS:

1. Add wet ingredients into the bowl and blend it with a stand mixer.
2. Add dry ingredients to another bowl and mix it well. Combine both dry and wet ingredients.
3. Fold into dried cranberries or chocolate chips. Divide the batter into two baskets.
4. Place air fryer basket to the Ninja foodi air fryer.
5. Select the "air fry" mode for Zone 1 with 165 degrees C temperature and 35-45 minutes of cooking time.
6. Press the "MATCH COOK" button to copy the setting for Zone 2.
7. Initiate cooking by pressing the "START/PAUSE" button.
8. When done, remove bread from the Ninja foodi air fryer.
9. Serve with jam or honey or butter.

Nutrition:

CALORIES: 336KCAL | FAT: 15G | CARBOHYDRATE: 1G | SUGAR: 31G | FIBER: 1G | PROTEIN: 3G

FISH AND SEAFOOD

SALMON CAKES

 **PREPARATION TIME** 10 MINUTES

 **COOKING TIME** 10 MINUTES

 **SERVINGS** 4 PERSONS

Ingredients:

- Salmon, 1lb, deboned
- Eggs, two
- Mayonnaise, 14ml
- Bell pepper red, ½
- Breadcrumbs, 64g
- Garlic powder, 2g
- Black pepper, 2g
- Salt, 1g
- Parsley, 28g, chopped
- Olive oil spray, 5g

Preparations:

1. Combine seasonings, egg, salmon, and breadcrumbs into the bowl.
2. Make patties from the mixture.
3. Divide the patties into two baskets.
4. Select the "air fry" mode for Zone 1 with 198 degrees C temperature and 10 minutes of cooking time.
5. Press the "MATCH COOK" button to copy the setting for Zone 2.
6. Initiate cooking by pressing the "START/PAUSE" button.
7. When done, remove and serve!

Nutrition:

CALORIES: 273KCAL | FAT: 13G | CARBOHYDRATE: 11G | PROTEIN: 26G | FIBER 1G | SUGAR 2G

SWAI FISH

 **PREPARATION TIME** 5 MINUTES

 **COOKING TIME** 10 MINUTES

 **SERVINGS** 2 PERSONS

Ingredients:

- Swai filets, 1lb
- Olive oil, 5ml
- Blackened seasoning, to taste

Preparations:

1. Brush olive oil on each side of fish fillets and season with blackened seasoning.
2. Divide the fish fillets into two baskets.
3. Select the "air fry" mode for Zone 1 with 198 degrees C temperature and 10 minutes of cooking time.
4. Press the "MATCH COOK" button to copy the setting for Zone 2.
5. Initiate cooking by pressing the "START/PAUSE" button.
6. When done, serve!

Nutrition:

CALORIES: 100KCAL | FAT: 1G | IRON: 1G | PROTEIN: 21G | CALCIUM | 1MG

COCONUT SHRIMP WITH DIPPING SAUCE

 **PREPARATION TIME** 10 MINUTES

 **COOKING TIME** 10 MINUTES

 **SERVINGS** 4 PERSONS

Ingredients:

- Raw shrimp, 1lb, peeled and deveined with tail on
- Eggs, 2, beaten
- Flour, 64g
- Unsweetened coconut, 64g, shredded
- Panko Breadcrumbs, 32g
- Salt, 5g
- Black pepper, 1g

Preparations:

1. Rinse and dry the shrimp and keep it aside.
2. Add flour in one bowl. Add egg in another bowl and beat it well.
3. Mix black pepper, salt, breadcrumbs, and coconut in 3rd bowl.
4. Immerse shrimp in flour and then dredge in egg. After that, dip in coconut mixture until covered.
5. Divide shrimps into two baskets.
6. Select the "air fry" mode for Zone 1 with 198 degrees C temperature and 10 minutes of cooking time.
7. Press the "MATCH COOK" button to copy the setting for Zone 2.
8. Initiate cooking by pressing the "START/PAUSE" button.
9. When done, remove and serve!

Nutrition:

CALORIES: 293KCAL | FAT: 11G | CARBOHYDRATE: 17G | PROTEIN: 28G | FIBER 2G | SUGAR 1G

JUMBO SHRIMP

 **PREPARATION TIME** 10 MINUTES

 **COOKING TIME** 10 MINUTES

 **SERVINGS** 4-5 PERSONS

Ingredients:

- Jumbo shrimp, 15, deveined, rinsed and pat dried
- Olive oil, 14ml
- Soy sauce, 22ml
- Garlic, 14g, minced
- Sugar, 7g
- Italian seasoning, 5g
- Ground black pepper, 5g
- White sesame seeds, 5g, for garnish
- Coriander, 28g, for garnish

Spicy Mayo Sauce:

- Mayonnaise, 59ml
- Sriracha, 14ml
- Lime juice, 14ml

Preparations:

1. Remove veins and rinse under clean water. Then, pat dry it with a paper towel.
2. Add shrimp into the mixing bowl. Then, add black pepper, Italian seasoning, sugar, garlic, soy sauce, and olive oil. Cover the bowl. Let rest for 20 minutes.
3. Divide the shrimps into two baskets.
4. Select the "air fry" mode for Zone 1 with 176 degrees C temperature and 10-15 minutes of cooking time.
5. Press the "MATCH COOK" button to copy the setting for Zone 2.
6. Initiate cooking by pressing the "START/PAUSE" button.
7. Meanwhile, prepare spicy mayo sauce: Mix the lime juice, sriracha, and mayonnaise into the bowl.
8. When done, transfer the shrimps onto the plate. Top with sesame seeds, fresh coriander, and mayonnaise sauce over it.

Nutrition:

CALORIES: 107KCAL | FAT: 5.5G | CARBOHYDRATE: 4.8G | PROTEIN: 10.5G | SUGAR 2.6G

PRAWNS

 **PREPARATION TIME** 10 MINUTES

 **COOKING TIME** 8 MINUTES

 **SERVINGS** 4 PERSONS

Ingredients:

- King prawns, 400g, peeled, uncooked
- Onion, ½, chopped
- Garlic, 2 cloves, chopped
- Olive oil, 29ml
- Lemon, ½, to serve
- Sea salt and black pepper, 1 pinch

Preparations:

1. Let chop the parsley, garlic, and onion.
2. Add parsley, garlic, onions, and prawns into the big bowl. Combine it well. Let marinate for fifteen minutes.
3. Divide the prawn mixture into two baskets.
4. Select the "air fry" mode for Zone 1 with 220 degrees C temperature and 8 minutes of cooking time.
5. Press the "MATCH COOK" button to copy the setting for Zone 2.
6. Initiate cooking by pressing the "START/PAUSE" button.
7. When done, squeeze lemon juice over it.

Nutrition:

CALORIES: 317KCAL | FAT: 17G | CARBOHYDRATE: 6G | PROTEIN: 42G | FIBER 1G | SUGAR 2G

MUSSELS

 **PREPARATION TIME** 10 MINUTES    **COOKING TIME** 5 MINUTES    **SERVINGS** 4 PERSONS

Ingredients:

- Mussels, 1 lb
- Butter, 14ml
- Water, 236ml
- Garlic, 10g, minced
- Chives, 5g
- Basil, 5g
- Parsley, 5g

Preparations:

1. Let soak mussels for 30 minutes. Then, clean it with a brush and discard the beard.
2. Mix the mussels, parsley, basil, chives, butter, garlic, and water into the bowl.
3. Divide the mussel mixture into two baskets.
4. Select the "air fry" mode for Zone 1 with 220 degrees C temperature and 5 minutes of cooking time.
5. Press the "MATCH COOK" button to copy the setting for Zone 2.
6. Initiate cooking by pressing the "START/PAUSE" button.
7. When done, remove and serve!

Nutrition:

CALORIES: 223KCAL | FAT: 3G | CARBOHYDRATE: 9G | PROTEIN: 27G | FIBER 0G | SUGAR 0G

COD NUGGETS

 **PREPARATION TIME** 5 MINUTES

 **COOKING TIME** 12 MINUTES

 **SERVINGS** 4 PERSONS

Ingredients:

- Cod, 1 lb
- Flour, 32g
- Salt, 2g
- Black pepper, 2g
- Egg, 2
- Breadcrumbs panko, 128g
- Garlic powder, 2g
- Greek yogurt plain, 170g
- Dill fresh, 28g, chopped
- Lemon, 1, juiced

Preparations:

1. Cut cod into pieces.
2. Mix the pepper, salt, and flour in a bowl. Whisk two eggs in another bowl. Mix garlic powder and panko in 3rd bowl.
3. Immerse cod pieces in flour mixture then in egg. Then, immerse in panko mixture.
4. Divide the mixture into two baskets.
5. Select the "air fry" mode for Zone 1 with 200 degrees C temperature and 10-12 minutes of cooking time.
6. Press the "MATCH COOK" button to copy the setting for Zone 2.
7. Initiate cooking by pressing the "START/PAUSE" button.
8. When done, serve with yogurt sauce.

Nutrition:

CARBOHYDRATES: 17G | PROTEIN: 24G | FAT: 5G | POTASSIUM: 97MG | FIBER: 1G

BLACK COD WITH BLACK BEAN SAUCE

 **PREPARATION TIME** 15 MINUTES

 **COOKING TIME** 17 MINUTES

 **SERVINGS** 2 PERSONS

Ingredients:

Black Cod:
- Black cod, 400g, cut into 2 steaks
- Garlic clove, 14g, minced
- Soy sauce, 5g
- Granulated sugar, 2g
- Salt, 2g
- Ground black pepper, 2g
- Coriander and jalapeno, for garnish

Black Bean Sauce:
- Black beans, 7g
- Water, 14ml
- Maggi sauce, 5ml
- Sesame oil, 2ml

Preparations:

1. Add pepper, salt, sugar, soy sauce, and garlic into the zip-lock bag and combine. Then, add cod steaks to it. Let marinate it for 30 minutes.
2. Divide the mixture into two baskets.
3. Select the "air fry" mode for Zone 1 with 176 degrees C temperature and 17 minutes of cooking time.
4. Press the "MATCH COOK" button to copy the setting for Zone 2.
5. Initiate cooking by pressing the "START/PAUSE" button.
6. Meanwhile, prepare black bean sauce: Mix the sesame oil, Maggi sauce, water, and black beans into the bowl and stir well.
7. When cod is prepared, remove and serve with black bean sauce.

Nutrition:

CALORIES: 194KCAL | FAT: 1.8G | CARBOHYDRATE: 8.6G | PROTEIN: 36.8G | SUGAR 4.3G

TUNA STEAKS

 **PREPARATION TIME** 20 MINUTES

 **COOKING TIME** 5 MINUTES

 **SERVINGS** 2 PERSONS

Ingredients:

- Tuna steaks, 170g, boneless, skinless
- Soy sauce, 59ml
- Honey, 10ml
- Ginger, 5g, grated
- Sesame oil, 5ml
- Rice vinegar, 2ml
- Green onions, sliced, to garnish
- Sesame seeds, to garnish

Preparations:

1. Mix the rice vinegar, sesame oil, grated ginger, honey, and soy sauce into the bowl. Add tuna steaks and let marinate for 20 to 30 minutes. Place it into the refrigerator.
2. Divide the mixture into two baskets.
3. Select the "air fry" mode for Zone 1 with 193 degrees C temperature and 5 minutes of cooking time.
4. Press the "MATCH COOK" button to copy the setting for Zone 2.
5. Initiate cooking by pressing the "START/PAUSE" button.
6. Garnish with sesame seeds and green onion.

Nutrition:

CALORIES: 422KCAL | FAT: 23G | CARBOHYDRATE: 8G | PROTEIN: 44G | SUGAR 6G

CAJUN SEASONED FRIED CATFISH

 **PREPARATION TIME** 30 MINUTES

 **COOKING TIME** 20 MINUTES

 **SERVINGS** 2 PERSONS

Ingredients:

- Catfish fillets, 1 pound
- Hot sauce, few dashes
- Yellow cornmeal, 64g
- Flour, 29g
- Cajun seasoning, 5g
- Lemon pepper seasoning, 2g
- Salt and fresh cracked black pepper, to taste
- Tartar sauce, hot sauce, lemon wedges, to serve

Preparations:

1. Add the hot sauce to the bowl. Then, add catfish fillets and coat them well. Let soak for 30 minutes.
2. Meanwhile, add seasonings, black pepper, flour, and cornmeal into the tray or plate and mix it well.
3. Remove catfish fillets from the hot sauce and season with salt.
4. Dredge in cornmeal mixture and coat it well.
5. Divide the mixture into two baskets.
6. Select the "air fry" mode for Zone 1 with 200 degrees C temperature and 20 minutes of cooking time.
7. Press the "MATCH COOK" button to copy the setting for Zone 2.
8. Initiate cooking by pressing the "START/PAUSE" button.
9. When done, serve with hot sauce, tartar sauce, and lemon wedges.

Nutrition:

CALORIES: 208KCAL | CARBOHYDRATES: 8G | PROTEIN: 17G | FAT: 9G

CAJUN SEASONED FRIED CATFISH | 27

PORK LETTUCE WRAPS

 **PREPARATION TIME** 10 MINUTES

 **COOKING TIME** 10 MINUTES

 **SERVINGS** 4 PERSONS

INGREDIENTS:

- Pork tenderloin, 1lb, cut into 1/2 inch slices
- Chili sauce, 59ml
- Soy sauce, 59ml, low-sodium
- Scallions, three, chopped
- Cooked brown rice, 256g
- Butter lettuce leaves, 12
- English cucumber, 128g, thinly sliced
- Carrots, 128g, shredded
- Sesame seeds, 7g
- Onions, two, sliced

PREPARATIONS:

1. Add pork pieces into the bowl. Then, add soy sauce and chili sauce and toss to combine. Cover the bowl with plastic wrap. Let marinate for 2 hours in the refrigerator.
2. Divide the pork pieces into two baskets.
3. Select the "air fry" mode for Zone 1 with 200 degrees C temperature and 10 minutes of cooking time.
4. Press the "MATCH COOK" button to copy the setting for Zone 2.
5. Initiate cooking by pressing the "START/PAUSE" button.
6. When done, remove and serve!

Nutrition:

CALORIES: 607KCAL | CARBOHYDRATES: 19G | PROTEIN: 34G | FAT: 44G

BEEF MEATLOAF

 **PREPARATION TIME** 10 MINUTES

 **COOKING TIME** 25 MINUTES

 **SERVINGS** 4 PERSONS

INGREDIENTS:

- Lean ground beef, 1lb
- Egg, 1, beaten
- Dry bread crumbs, 42g
- Onion, 1, chopped
- Fresh thyme, 14g, chopped
- Salt, 5g
- Ground black pepper, to taste
- Mushrooms, 2, thickly sliced
- Olive oil, 14ml

PREPARATIONS:

1. Mix the pepper, thyme, salt, onion, egg, breadcrumbs, and ground beef into the bowl. Then, knead and combine it well.
2. Let smooth it with your hand and press mushrooms in it. Then, coat with olive oil.
3. Place it into the air fryer basket.
4. Select the "air fry" mode for Zone 1 with 200 degrees C temperature and 25 minutes of cooking time.
5. Press the "MATCH COOK" button to copy the setting for Zone 2.
6. Initiate cooking by pressing the "START/PAUSE" button.
7. When done, remove and serve!

Nutrition:

CALORIES: 297KCAL | CARBOHYDRATES: 5.9G | PROTEIN: 24G | FAT: 18.8G

PORK CHOP BITES WITH MUSHROOMS

 **PREPARATION TIME** 15 MINUTES   **COOKING TIME** 15 MINUTES   **SERVINGS** 4 PERSONS

INGREDIENTS:

- Pork belly or pork chops, 1lb, rinsed and pat dry
- Mushrooms, 226g, cleaned, washed and halved
- Butter, 30ml, melted
- Worcestershire sauce or soy sauce, 5ml
- Garlic powder, 2g
- Salt and black pepper, to taste

PREPARATIONS:

1. Cut pork chops into cubes and mix with mushrooms.
2. Then, coat with oil or butter. Sprinkle with pepper, salt, garlic powder, and Worcestershire sauce.
3. Divide the pork and mushrooms mixture into two baskets.
4. Select the "air fry" mode for Zone 1 with 200 degrees C temperature and 10-18 minutes of cooking time.
5. Press the "MATCH COOK" button to copy the setting for Zone 2.
6. Initiate cooking by pressing the "START/PAUSE" button.
7. When done, remove and serve!

Nutrition:

CALORIES: 241KCAL | CARBOHYDRATES: 2G | PROTEIN: 26G | FAT: 14G

STUFFED ZUCCHINI BOATS WITH SAUSAGE

 **PREPARATION TIME** 20 MINUTES

 **COOKING TIME** 10 MINUTES

 **SERVINGS** 4 PERSONS

INGREDIENTS:

- Zucchini, 2, halved and cored
- Uncooked sausage meat, ½ lb
- Breadcrumbs, 32g
- Cheese, 57g, grated
- Parsley, 2 8g, chopped

PREPARATIONS:

1. Firstly, halve and core the zucchini. Place zucchini onto the clean work surface and spray with olive oil.
2. Flip the zucchini and stuff with sausage meat and top with cheese and breadcrumbs.
3. Divide the stuffed zucchini into two baskets.
4. Select the "air fry" mode for Zone 1 with 180 degrees C temperature and 10-14 minutes of cooking time.
5. Press the "MATCH COOK" button to copy the setting for Zone 2.
6. Initiate cooking by pressing the "START/PAUSE" button.
7. Garnish with parsley leaves.

Nutrition:

CALORIES: 285KCAL | CARBOHYDRATES: 9G | PROTEIN: 16G | FAT: 21G

BROWN SUGAR AND HONEY GLAZED HAM

 **PREPARATION TIME** 5 MINUTES
 **COOKING TIME** 55 MINUTES
 **SERVINGS** 12 PERSONS

INGREDIENTS:

- Ham, 4lbs, cooked, boneless

Brown sugar glaze:
- Brown sugar, 110g
- Honey, 60ml
- Orange juice, 60ml
- Apple cider vinegar, 60ml
- Cinnamon, 1g
- Clove, 32g
- Black pepper, to taste

PREPARATIONS:

To prepare the glaze:

1. Add honey and brown sugar glaze ingredients into the saucepan and heat, and whisk it well until combined. Keep it aside.
2. Brush the glaze over the ham. Wrap the ham with foil.
3. Divide ham into two baskets.
4. Select the "air fry" mode for Zone 1 with 150 degrees C temperature and 20 minutes of cooking time.
5. Press the "MATCH COOK" button to copy the setting for Zone 2.
6. Initiate cooking by pressing the "START/PAUSE" button.
7. Open the foil, brush the ham with glaze. Close the foil. Return to Ninja air fryer. Adjust the temperature to 150 degrees C and cooking time for 20 minutes more.
8. Open the foil, brush with more and return to ninja foodi Air fryer. Adjust the temperature to 180 degrees C and cooking time for 5 minutes.
9. When done, remove and serve!

Nutrition:

CALORIES: 428KCAL | CARBOHYDRATES: 16G | PROTEIN: 33G | FAT: 25G

PORK CHOPS PARMIGIANA

 **PREPARATION TIME** 10 MINUTES  **COOKING TIME** 18 MINUTES  **SERVINGS** 3 PERSONS

INGREDIENTS:

- Pork chops, 170g, rinsed and patted dry
- Salt and black pepper, to taste
- Garlic powder and smoked paprika, to taste
- Breadcrumbs, 54g
- Parmesan cheese, 50g, grated
- Parsley, 28g, chopped
- Egg, 1
- Mozzarella cheese, 56g
- Marinara sauce, 240ml

PREPARATIONS:

1. Firstly, season the pork chops with paprika, garlic powder, pepper, and salt.
2. Combine the chopped parsley, parmesan cheese, and breadcrumbs in a bowl. Add egg in another bowl and beat it well.
3. Immerse each pork chop in egg and then in the breadcrumb mixture until coated.
4. Select the "air fry" mode for Zone 1 with 194 degrees C temperature and 8-12 minutes of cooking time.
5. Press the "MATCH COOK" button to copy the setting for Zone 2.
6. Initiate cooking by pressing the "START/PAUSE" button.
7. Open the lid, top with cheese and cook for two minutes more.
8. Serve with marinara sauce.

Nutrition:

CALORIES: 495KCAL | CARBOHYDRATES: 18G | PROTEIN: 53G | FAT: 22G

ROAST LAMB

 **PREPARATION TIME** 10 MINUTES  **COOKING TIME** 1 HOUR 20 MINUTES  **SERVINGS** 4 PERSONS

INGREDIENTS:

Lamb:
- Leg of lamb, 3lbs, boneless
- Garlic, 3 cloves
- Olive oil, 29ml
- Sea salt, 2g
- Cracked pepper, 1g

Mint sauce glaze:
- Mint leaves, 43g, chopped
- Brown sugar, 28g
- Malt vinegar, 36ml
- Water, 29ml, boiled
- Salt, 5g

PREPARATIONS:

1. Pat the lamb dry with a paper towel. Cut slits into the skin with a sharp knife. Cut garlic into slivers and insert one piece into each slice.
2. Drizzle the lamb with olive oil and sprinkle with pepper and salt.
3. Divide the lamb mixture into two baskets.
4. Select the "air fry" mode for Zone 1 with 194 degrees C temperature and 20 minutes of cooking time.
5. Press the "MATCH COOK" button to copy the setting for Zone 2.
6. Initiate cooking by pressing the "START/PAUSE" button.
7. Meanwhile, add salt, brown sugar, and boiled water into the mixing bowl and stir well. Let chop the mint and then add to the mixing bowl. Add malt vinegar and combine it well. Keep it aside.
8. Open the lid, baste the lamb with a mint glaze and cook for twenty minutes.
9. Baste the lamb every 20 minutes until you get desired consistency.
10. When done, let rest for ten to 15 minutes.
11. Serve and enjoy!

Nutrition:

CALORIES: 406KCAL | CARBOHYDRATES: 9G | PROTEIN: 46G | FAT: 19G

GREEK LAMB BURGERS

 **PREPARATION TIME** 10 MINUTES    **COOKING TIME** 20 MINUTES    **SERVINGS** 4 PERSONS

INGREDIENTS:

- Ground lamb, 1 ½ lbs
- Oregano, 5g
- Feta cheese, 43g, crumbled
- Salt and pepper, 2g
- Buns, 4
- Lettuce, ½ head
- Tomato, 1
- Greek yogurt, 236ml

PREPARATIONS:

1. Combine pepper, crumbled feta cheese, oregano, and ground lamb into the bowl. Make patties. Season with pepper and salt.
2. Place burgers into the air fryer basket.
3. Select the "air fry" mode for Zone 1 with 190 degrees C temperature and 8-10 minutes of cooking time.
4. Press the "MATCH COOK" button to copy the setting for Zone 2.
5. Initiate cooking by pressing the "START/PAUSE" button.
6. When done, remove the burger from the Ninja foodi air fryer.
7. Let rest for five minutes.
8. Top burger with tomato slices, lettuce leaves, yogurt.

Nutrition:

CALORIES: 790KCAL | CARBOHYDRATES: 40G | PROTEIN: 38G | FAT: 21G

LAMB MEATBALLS

 **PREPARATION TIME** 10 MINUTES    **COOKING TIME** 20 MINUTES    **SERVINGS** 15 PERSONS

INGREDIENTS:

- Ground lamb, 1lb
- Red bell pepper, 1, diced
- Red onion, 43g, diced
- Cilantro, 43g, diced
- Zucchini, 43g, diced
- Greek seasoning, 14g
- Turmeric, 2g
- Cumin, 2g
- Coriander, 2g
- Garlic cloves, 2, minced
- Salt and pepper, to taste

PREPARATIONS:

1. Add veggies into the blender and blend a couple of times.
2. Cook veggies in ghee for five to seven minutes. Let cool it.
3. Season lamb with Greek seasoning, garlic, pepper, salt, coriander, and turmeric.
4. Add cooked veggies to the lamb mixture and combine it with your hands. Make into meatballs with your hand.
5. Divide the meatballs into two baskets.
6. Select the "air fry" mode for Zone 1 with 187 degrees C temperature and 15 minutes of cooking time.
7. Press the "MATCH COOK" button to copy the setting for Zone 2.
8. Initiate cooking by pressing the "START/PAUSE" button.
9. When done, serve and enjoy!

Nutrition:

CALORIES: 524KCAL | CARBOHYDRATES: 21G | PROTEIN: 39G | FAT: 32G

PORK SCHNITZEL

 **PREPARATION TIME** 10 MINUTES    **COOKING TIME** 15 MINUTES    **SERVINGS** 4 PERSONS

INGREDIENTS:

- Pork chops, 4, boneless, cut or pounded to 1/3" thickness
- Thyme, 1g
- Garlic salt, 1/2g
- Fajita seasoning, 1g
- Dried sage, 1g
- Rosemary, 1g, minced
- Egg, 1
- Flour, 64g
- Salt and pepper, to taste
- Panko, 85g

PREPARATIONS:

1. Rinse and pat dry the pork chops.
2. Mix panko and spices into the bowl. Add pepper and salt.
3. Add egg into another bowl. Add flour in 3rd bowl.
4. Immerse chop in flour and then dip in egg wash. Then, dredge into the panko mixture.
5. Place pork chops into the basket.
6. Select the "air fry" mode for Zone 1 with 198 degrees C temperature and 12-14 minutes of cooking time.
7. Press the "MATCH COOK" button to copy the setting for Zone 2.
8. Initiate cooking by pressing the "START/PAUSE" button.
9. When done, remove and serve!

Nutrition:

CALORIES: 461KCAL | CARBOHYDRATES: 25G | PROTEIN: 42G | FAT: 21G

BEEF AND BROCCOLI

 **PREPARATION TIME** 60 MINUTES

 **COOKING TIME** 15 MINUTES

 **SERVINGS** 4 PERSONS

INGREDIENTS:

- 455 g flank steak, sliced
- ½ tsp ginger, grated
- 3 garlic cloves, minced
- 2 tbsp water
- 30 ml (2 tbsp) sesame oil
- 80 ml (5 tbsp) low sodium soy sauce
- 240 ml beef broth
- 700 g broccoli florets
- 55g brown sugar
- 85 g honey
- 2 tbsp corn starch

PREPARATIONS:

1. Take a medium-sized bowl, mix all the ingredients—Allow marinating for an hour.
2. Place them in the air fryer basket and broccoli in the other basket and cook for 15 minutes at 176 degrees C.
3. Serve beef with broccoli white rice and garnish with sesame seeds. Enjoy!

Nutrition:

CALORIES: 556KCAL | CARBOHYDRATES: 60G | PROTEIN: 37G | FAT: 18G | SUGAR 35G

STEAK BITES WITH GARLIC BUTTER

 **PREPARATION TIME**
10 MINUTES

 COOKING TIME
10 MINUTES

 SERVINGS
4 PERSONS

INGREDIENTS:

- 21g butter
- ¼ red pepper flakes
- ¼ tsp garlic powder
- ¼ tsp parsley flakes
- 455g flank steak, cut into bite-sized pieces
- 6 g brown sugar
- 8 g olive oil
- 1 tsp chili powder
- 1 tsp kosher salt and black pepper
- ¼ tsp garlic powder
- ¼ tsp onion powder

PREPARATIONS:

1. Grab a bowl, rub olive oil, brown sugar, and other spices on the steak. Allow marinating for few minutes.
2. Place steak bites on air fry basket. Air fry for 5 minutes at 400 degrees F.
3. Meanwhile, melt butter and whisk with parsley, red pepper, and garlic powder.
4. Toss the steak with garlic butter. serve and enjoy!

Nutrition:

CALORIES: 200KCAL | CARBOHYDRATES: 1G | PROTEIN: 25G | FAT: 10G

STEAK BITES WITH MUSHROOMS

 **PREPARATION TIME** 10 MINUTES   **COOKING TIME** 20 MINUTES    **SERVINGS** 4 PERSONS

INGREDIENTS:

- 455 g steaks
- 227 g mushrooms
- 1 tsp Worcestershire sauce
- 21 g butter
- 1 ½ tsp garlic powder
- Kosher salt and Black pepper, to taste
- Parsley, minced
- Chili flakes and Melted butter

PREPARATIONS:

1. Take a large-sized bowl, mix mushrooms and steak with butter, sauce, salt, pepper, and garlic powder.
2. Preheat the air fryer for 5 minutes at 200 degrees C
3. Place steak bites in one basket of the air fryer. Now place mushrooms in the second basket. Air fry for 10 minutes.
4. Place mushrooms and steak bites in the serving dish together. Drizzle melted butter and sprinkle chili flakes, salt and butter, and parsley. Enjoy!

Nutrition:

CALORIES: 300KCAL | CARBOHYDRATES: 2G | PROTEIN: 24G | FAT: 21G

BEEF ROAST AND POTATO FRIES

 **PREPARATION TIME** 5 MINUTES

 **COOKING TIME** 45 MINUTES

 **SERVINGS** 6 PERSONS

INGREDIENTS:

- 904 g beef (2 beef roast)
- 1 onion
- 2 tsp thyme
- 1 tbsp olive oil
- 1 tsp salt and Black pepper
- 1 large-sized potato

PREPARATIONS:

1. Take a large-sized bowl, rub beef roast with salt, oil, and thyme.
2. Peel onion and cut into halves. Then peel the potato and slice it.
3. Preheat the air fryer at 200 degrees C for 5 minutes. Place onions and beef roast into the air fryer basket. Place fries into another basket of the air fryer.
4. Air fry until cooked through.
5. Allow beef to cool for 10 minutes before serving.
6. Serve beef with vegetables and fries, and enjoy!

Nutrition:

CALORIES: 200KCAL | CARBOHYDRATES: 4G | PROTEIN: 36G | FAT: 9G

BURGERS

 **PREPARATION TIME** 10 MINUTES

 **COOKING TIME** 10 MINUTES

 **SERVINGS** 4 PERSONS

INGREDIENTS:

FOR BURGERS

- 455 g beef, grounded
- 1 tsp garlic, minced
- 1 tsp salt and black pepper
- ½ red onion, diced
- 1tsp hot English mustard
- 1 tsp Worcestershire sauce

FOR BURGERS BUNS

- 1 tsp baking powder
- 2 tbsp oat fiber
- 6 tbsp baking blend
- ¼ tsp salt
- 1/8 tsp garlic powder
- 1/8 tsp onion powder
- 6 tbsp egg whites
- ¼ cup water
- 1 tsp oil
- 1 tbsp apple cider vinegar

PREPARATIONS:

1. Preheat 2 baskets air fryer to 177 degrees C.
2. Take a large mixing bowl, mix all burger ingredients. Form patties of your desired size from the mixture.
3. Take another mixing bowl, mix bun ingredients.
4. Prepare the baking pan, pour the batter into the baking pan.
5. Place burgers in one basket of Air fryer and buns pan into another basket—air fry beef burgers and buns for 10 minutes.
6. Place burgers between two buns and top with your favourite toppings. Serve and enjoy!

Nutrition:

CALORIES: 215KCAL | CARBOHYDRATES: 3G | PROTEIN: 19G | FAT: 12G

TAQUITOS WITH GREEN BEANS

 **PREPARATION TIME**
15 MINUTES

 **COOKING TIME**
10 MINUTES

 **SERVINGS**
4 PERSONS

INGREDIENTS:

FOR TAQUITOS:
- 455 lean ground beef
- 2 large eggs
- 10 corn tortillas
- 3 tbsp taco seasoning
- 60 g bread crumbs

FOR BEANS:
- 450 g green beans
- 1 tbsp olive oil
- Salt, pepper, and garlic powder, to taste

PREPARATIONS:

1. Preheat the air fryer at 177 degrees C.
2. Take a large-sized bowl, mix beef, eggs, taco seasoning, and bread crumbs.
3. Spoon 25 g beef mixture into each tortilla. Now roll up and secure ends with toothpicks.
4. Now, arrange taquitos in one basket of the air fryer.
5. Take another bowl, mix beans with olive oil, garlic powder, salt, and pepper.
6. Lace green beans in the second basket of the air fryer.
7. Air fry for 10 minutes. serve warm and enjoy!

Nutrition:

CALORIES: 195KCAL | CARBOHYDRATES: 20G | PROTEIN: 15G | FAT: 8G

BEEF WITH RATATOUILLE

 **PREPARATION TIME** 25 MINUTES
 **COOKING TIME** 20 MINUTES
 **SERVINGS** 2 PERSONS

INGREDIENTS:

FOR STEAK:

- 2 beef steaks (750 g)
- 1 tsp each salt, pepper, and paprika
- 1 tbsp onion powder
- 1 tbsp garlic powder
- 2 tbsp herbs, dried

FOR RATATOUILLE:

- ¼ small eggplant, cubed
- ¼ onion, cubed
- ½ tomato, cubed
- ¼ zucchini, cubed
- ¼ each red and yellow bell pepper, cut into cubes
- ½ cayenne pepper, diced
- ½ tbsp olive oil
- ½ tbsp white wine
- ½ garlic clove, crushed
- Basil and oregano, as desired
- Salt and pepper, to taste

PREPARATIONS:

1. Preheat the air fryer at 200 degrees C.
2. Rub steaks with olive oil and set aside. Take a bowl, mix salt, pepper, onion powder, garlic powder, paprika, and dried herbs.
3. Coat steaks with desired seasonings.
4. Take a bowl, place all ratatouille ingredients in it. Mix until all the vegetables are coated well.
5. Pour the vegetable mixture into the baking dish.
6. Place steak in one basket and ratatouille in another basket of the air fryer. Air fry for 10 minutes (flip frequently).
7. Serve beef steaks with ratatouille and enjoy our perfect meal.

Nutrition:

CALORIES: 500KCAL | CARBOHYDRATES: 15.5G | PROTEIN: 67G | FAT: 21G

GARLIC LAMB CHOPS WITH ROSEMARY POTATO WEDGES

 **PREPARATION TIME** 40 MINUTES

 COOKING TIME 10 MINUTES

 SERVINGS 4 PERSONS

INGREDIENTS:

LAMB CHOPS

- 540 g rack of lamb, about 8 chops
- 3 tbsp (45 ml) olive oil
- 1 tsp (5 ml) garlic powder
- 1 tsp (5 ml) salt and black pepper
- 2 tbsp (30 ml) rosemary, chopped

FOR POTATO WEDGES

- 12 wedges of russet potatoes
- 1 tbsp EVOO
- 2 tsp seasoned salt
- 1 tsp rosemary

PREPARATIONS:

1. Take a large bowl, mix salt, oil, rosemary, garlic, and pepper. Rub the mixture over lamb chops and allow to marinate for some time.
2. Take another bowl, mix potato wedges with seasoned salt, oil, and rosemary.
3. Place lamb chops in one basket of air fryers and potato wedges in another air fryer basket.
4. Air fry for 20 minutes at 177 degrees C (flip and check frequently).
5. Serve rosemary lamb chops with rosemary potato wedges.

Nutrition:

CALORIES: 505KCAL | CARBOHYDRATES: 21G | PROTEIN: 31G | FAT: 37G

LAMB SHANKS WITH BUTTERNUT SQUASH FRIES

 **PREPARATION TIME** 15 MINUTES
 COOKING TIME 50 MINUTES
 SERVINGS 4 PERSONS

INGREDIENTS:

FOR LAMB SHANKS

- 4 lamb shanks
- 2 tsp olive oil
- 2 tsp garlic, crushed
- 2 tsp salt and pepper
- 1 tsp rosemary leaves
- 2 tsp oregano
- 250 ml stock

FOR BUTTERNUT SQUASH FRIES

- 1 large peeled butternut squash, sliced into "fries"
- 1 tablespoon olive oil
- ½ tablespoon Chinese five-spice powder
- ½ tablespoon garlic, minced
- 2 teaspoons sea salt and Black pepper

PREPARATIONS:

1. Preheat air fryer at 190 degrees C.
2. Take a bowl, mix squash with salt, pepper, garlic, and five-spice powder. Toss to coat well.
3. Take another large bowl, mix oil, salt, pepper, garlic, rosemary, and oregano. Rub the lamb shanks with this mixture.
4. Now, place squash fries in one basket and lamb shank in another basket of the air fryer.
5. Air fry for 20 minutes. Then remove butternut squash fries from the air fryer.
6. Add stock in lamb shanks basket of the air fryer. Air fry for 30 minutes.
7. Serve and enjoy lamb shank with butternut squash fries.

Nutrition:

CALORIES: 357KCAL | CARBOHYDRATES: 4G | PROTEIN: 56G | FAT: 16G

TONKATSU WITH WHITE RICE

 **PREPARATION TIME** 15 MINUTES  **COOKING TIME** 25 MINUTES  **SERVINGS** 2 PERSONS

INGREDIENTS:

FOR RICE
- 1 cup basmati rice
- 2 cups salted boiling water

FOR TONKATSU
- 450 g boneless pork, 4 chops
- Salt and Black pepper
- Tomato sauce
- 2 large eggs
- ¾ cup panko bread crumbs

PREPARATIONS:

1. Preheat the air fryer to 190 degrees C.
2. Season pork chops with salt and pepper. Take a small bowl, whisk eggs in it. Place bread crumbs in another dish.
3. First, dip chops with egg and then coat with bread crumbs. Place pork chops in the basket of the air fryer in a single layer.
4. Wash the rice with warm water. Add rice to the cake pan. Then add boiled water to the pan and tightly cover with aluminium. Place the pan in the second basket of the air fryer.
5. Now, air fry for 25 minutes. Serve tonkatsu with warm white rice and enjoy

Nutrition:

CALORIES: 324KCAL | CARBOHYDRATES: 65G | PROTEIN: 24G | FAT: 12G

BBQ PORK TENDERLOIN WITH MUSHROOMS

 **PREPARATION TIME** 15 MINUTES

 **COOKING TIME** 15 MINUTES

 **SERVINGS** 2 PERSONS

INGREDIENTS:

FOR BBQ PORK TENDERLOIN

- 285 grams Pork Tenderloin, diced
- 4 tbsp (1/4 cup) BBQ Sauce
- 1 tsp Olive Oil

FOR MUSHROOMS

- 225 g cremini mushrooms, halved
- 2 tbsp avocado oil
- 1 tsp low-sodium soy sauce
- ½ tsp garlic, chopped
- Salt and Black pepper

PREPARATIONS:

1. Toss the diced pork with sauce and olive oil—place in the basket of the air fryer.
2. In another bowl, mix mushrooms with oil, salt, pepper, garlic, and soy sauce—place mushrooms in the second basket of the air fryer.
3. Air fry for 20 minutes at 204 degrees C.
4. Serve spicy BBQ pork tenderloin with mushrooms.

Nutrition:
CALORIES: 365KCAL | CARBOHYDRATES: 17G | PROTEIN: 41G | FAT: 18G

PORK LOIN SANDWICH WITH GREEN TOMATOES

 PREPARATION TIME 25 MINUTES   **COOKING TIME** 20 MINUTES   **SERVINGS** 4 PERSONS

INGREDIENTS:

FOR PORK TENDERLOIN SANDWICH

- 2 boneless pork chops
- 1/2 cup all-purpose flour
- 2 large eggs lightly beaten
- 1 cup (120g) Panko bread crumbs
- Salt and pepper

FOR AIR-FRIED GREEN TOMATOES

- 2 green tomatoes, sliced
- Salt and black pepper
- 3 ½ tbsp all-purpose flour
- 60g buttermilk
- 2 egg
- 80g bread crumbs
- 90g yellow cornmeal
- 1g garlic powder
- 1g paprika

PREPARATIONS:

1. First, season tomato slices with salt and pepper.
2. Take 3 dishes, place the flour into the first dish, stir together eggs and buttermilk in the second dish, and mix paprika, breadcrumbs, garlic powder, and cornmeal in the third dish.
3. Now, coat tomato slices with flour, then dip into the egg mixture, and cover with bread crumbs mixture.
4. Place tomato slices in the air fryer basket. Brush olive oil on top of slices.
5. Take two bowls, place flour in one bowl, and whisk together salt, pepper, and eggs in the second bowl.
6. Coat pounded chops with flour and then coat with egg mixture.
7. Place pork chops into the second basket of the air fryer.
8. Now start the air fryer and cook for 20 minutes at 200 degrees C.
9. Now, place pork chops on a bun and top with green tomatoes, mayo, and other toppings. Serve warm and enjoy!

Nutrition:

CALORIES: 324KCAL | CARBOHYDRATES: 65G | PROTEIN: 24G | FAT: 12G

PORK SCHNITZEL AND POTATO HAY

 PREPARATION TIME 20 MINUTES   **COOKING TIME** 20 MINUTES   **SERVINGS** 4 PERSONS

INGREDIENTS:

FOR PORK SCHNITZEL

- 37g all-purpose flour
- 1 tsp seasoned salt and pepper
- 1 large egg
- 2 tbsp milk
- 89g dry bread crumbs
- 1 tsp paprika
- 4 pork sirloin cutlets (110g each), pounded
- 120 ml Dill sauce

FOR POTATO HAY

- 2 russet potatoes, cut into spirals and well-soaked
- 1 tbsp canola oil
- Salt and Black pepper

PREPARATIONS:

1. Preheat the air fryer to 200 degrees C.
2. Take a dish, mix salt, pepper, and flour. Take a second dish and whisk in milk and egg. Take a third bowl and mix paprika and bread crumbs.
3. Now, first coat pounded cutlets with flour mixture, then dip in egg mixture, and last coat with crumb mixture.
4. Place pork cutlets in a tray and place them in an air fryer basket.
5. Toss potato spirals with salt, pepper, and oil. Place spirals in the second basket of the air fryer.
6. Air fry for 20 minutes.
7. Serve pork schnitzel with dill sauce and potato hay.

Nutrition:

CALORIES: 345KCAL | CARBOHYDRATES: 27G | PROTEIN: 30G | FAT: 17G

POULTRY

YUMMY CHICKEN CUTLETS

 **PREPARATION TIME**
15 MINUTES

 **COOKING TIME**
8 MINUTES

 **SERVINGS**
2 PERSONS

Ingredients:

- Chicken cutlets, 2
- Panko breadcrumbs, 128g
- Garlic powder, 5g
- Salt, 5g
- Pepper, 1g
- Flour, 64g
- Eggs, 2, beaten

Preparations:

1. Add pepper, salt, garlic powder, and breadcrumbs into the bowl and mix it well.
2. Add flour to another bowl. Whisk eggs in 3rd bowl.
3. Season chicken cutlets with pepper and salt.
4. Dredge chicken cutlets in the flour, then immerse in flour and place into breadcrumbs, and coat on each side.
5. Divide coated chicken cutlets into two baskets.
6. Select the "air fry" mode for Zone 1 with 200 degrees C temperature and 8 minutes of cooking time.
7. Press the "MATCH COOK" button to copy the setting for Zone 2.
8. Initiate cooking by pressing the "START/PAUSE" button.
9. When done, serve and enjoy!

Nutrition:

CALORIES: 495KCAL | FAT: 11G | CARBOHYDRATE: 47G | SUGAR: 2G | FIBER: 2G | PROTEIN: 49G

POPCORN CHICKEN

 **PREPARATION TIME** 15 MINUTES    **COOKING TIME** 10 MINUTES    **SERVINGS** 6 PERSONS

Ingredients:

- Chicken breasts, 1lb, boneless, cut into bite size pieces
- Panko bread crumbs, 128g
- Flour, 128g
- Chili flakes, 5g
- Oregano, 10g
- Onion powder, 10g
- Garlic powder, 10g
- Pepper, 10g
- Salt, 10g
- Egg, 1

Preparations:

1. Rinse the chicken and pat it dry with a paper towel—season with oregano, garlic powder, onion powder, chili flakes, black pepper, and salt.
2. Let rest for 10 minutes.
3. Immerse chicken pieces into the flour and then immerse in the egg. Then, dredge in the breadcrumbs.
4. Divide coated chicken cutlets into two baskets.
5. Select the "air fry" mode for Zone 1 with 176 degrees C temperature and 10 minutes of cooking time.
6. Press the "MATCH COOK" button to copy the setting for Zone 2.
7. Initiate cooking by pressing the "START/PAUSE" button.
8. When done, remove popcorn chicken from the Ninja foodi air fryer.
9. Serve and enjoy!

Nutrition:

CALORIES: 253KCAL | FAT: 4G | CARBOHYDRATE: 31G | SUGAR: 1G | FIBER: 2G | PROTEIN: 22G

CHICKEN LEG QUARTERS

 **PREPARATION TIME**
5 MINUTES

 **COOKING TIME**
40 MINUTES

 **SERVINGS**
2 PERSONS

Ingredients:

- Chicken leg quarters, 2 pieces
- Salt and pepper, to taste
- Barbecue sauce, 59ml

Preparations:

1. Brush chicken legs with olive oil.
2. Season chicken legs with pepper and salt.
3. Divide chicken legs into two baskets.
4. Select the "air fry" mode for Zone 1 with 195 degrees C temperature and 35 minutes of cooking time.
5. Press the "MATCH COOK" button to copy the setting for Zone 2.
6. Initiate cooking by pressing the "START/PAUSE" button.
7. Open the lid and baste with BBQ sauce and close the lid.
8. When done, let rest for five minutes.
9. Serve and enjoy!

Nutrition:

CALORIES: 58KCAL | FAT: 1G | CARBOHYDRATE: 14G | SUGAR: 11G | FIBER: 1G | PROTEIN: 1G

CHICKEN BURGER

 **PREPARATION TIME** 10 MINUTES

 **COOKING TIME** 20 MINUTES

 **SERVINGS** 4 PERSONS

Ingredients:

- Ground chicken, 1lb
- Seasoned bread crumbs, 64g
- Parmesan cheese, 32g, grated
- Egg, 1, beaten
- Garlic, 14g, minced
- Worcestershire sauce, 5ml

Preparations:

1. Mix the Worcestershire sauce, garlic, egg, parmesan cheese, breadcrumbs, and ground chicken into the bowl.
2. Make patties from the mixture. Place it into the refrigerator for 15 minutes to 1 hour.
3. Divide chicken patties into two baskets.
4. Select the "air fry" mode for Zone 1 with 190 degrees C temperature and 18 minutes of cooking time.
5. Press the "MATCH COOK" button to copy the setting for Zone 2.
6. Initiate cooking by pressing the "START/PAUSE" button.
7. Place patties between the burger.

Nutrition:

CALORIES: 318KCAL | FAT: 16G | CARBOHYDRATE: 12.1G | PROTEIN: 32G

BARBEQUE CHICKEN SAUSAGE PIZZA

 PREPARATION TIME 10 MINUTES   **COOKING TIME** 6 MINUTES   **SERVINGS** 6 PERSONS

Ingredients:

- Naan bread, 1 piece
- Barbeque sauce, 59ml
- Mozzarella cheese, 32g
- Gouda cheese, 32g
- Red onion, 1/8, thinly sliced
- Chicken sausage, ½
- Fresh coriander, chopped

Preparations:

1. Place BBQ sauce over naan and top with red onion, Gouda cheese, and mozzarella cheese. Place chicken sausage over the pizza and spray with cooking spray.
2. Divide mixture into two baskets.
3. Select the "air fry" mode for Zone 1 with 200 degrees C temperature and 6-9 minutes of cooking time.
4. Press the "MATCH COOK" button to copy the setting for Zone 2.
5. Initiate cooking by pressing the "START/PAUSE" button.
6. When done, remove and serve!

Nutrition:

CALORIES: 643KCAL | FAT: 23G | CARBOHYDRATE: 76.3G | PROTEIN: 31G

BUFFALO CHICKEN CALZONES

 **PREPARATION TIME** 10 MINUTES   **COOKING TIME** 10 MINUTES    **SERVINGS** 4 PERSONS

Ingredients:

- Chicken, 171g, shredded
- Buffalo wing sauce, 59ml
- Mozzarella cheese, 171g, shredded
- Blue cheese crumbles, 32g
- Pizza crust, 1 tube, refrigerated
- Ranch dressing and green onion, to serve

Preparations:

1. Spread a sheet of pizza dough onto the clean work surface. Cut the dough into squares with a pizza cutter.
2. Cut each square into a circle with a pizza cutter.
3. Combine blue cheese crumbles, buffalo sauce, and chicken into the bowl—top one half of each circle of dough with shredded cheese and chicken.
4. Then, fold over the cheese and meat and seal it.
5. Spray each calzone with olive oil.
6. Divide calzones into two baskets.
7. Select the "air fry" mode for Zone 1 with 162 degrees C temperature and 8-10 minutes of cooking time.
8. Press the "MATCH COOK" button to copy the setting for Zone 2.
9. Initiate cooking by pressing the "START/PAUSE" button.
10. When done, remove from the Ninja air fryer.
11. Top with ranch dressing and green onions.

Nutrition:

CALORIES: 580KCAL | FAT: 22G | CARBOHYDRATE: 65G | PROTEIN: 29G | FIBER 3G

DELICIOUS CHICKEN MEATBALLS

 **PREPARATION TIME** 10 MINUTES

 **COOKING TIME** 15 MINUTES

 **SERVINGS** 4 PERSONS

Ingredients:

- Ground chicken breast, 1lb
- Breadcrumbs, 128g
- Egg, 1
- Italian seasoning, 14g
- Ground black pepper, 5g
- Parmesan cheese, 64g
- Marinara sauce, 177ml
- Mozzarella cheese, 64g, shredded

Preparations:

1. Combine the seasoning, egg, parmesan cheese, chicken, and breadcrumbs into the mixing bowl.
2. Shape mixture into meatballs.
3. Divide meatballs into two baskets.
4. Select the "air fry" mode for Zone 1 with 176 degrees C temperature and 15 minutes of cooking time.
5. Press the "MATCH COOK" button to copy the setting for Zone 2.
6. Initiate cooking by pressing the "START/PAUSE" button.
7. Open the lid, top with marinara sauce and mozzarella cheese.
8. Serve!

Nutrition:

CALORIES: 391KCAL | FAT: 18G | CARBOHYDRATE: 24G | PROTEIN: 33G | FIBER 3G

PISTACHIO CRUSTED CHICKEN

 **PREPARATION TIME** 5 MINUTES

 **COOKING TIME** 15 MINUTES

 **SERVINGS** 2 PERSONS

Ingredients:

- Chicken breast, 170g, skinless
- Salt, 2g
- Pepper, 1g
- Mayonnaise, 29ml
- Pistachios, 64g, roasted and salted
- Olive oil, 14ml

Preparations:

1. Season chicken breast with pepper and salt.
2. Top with one tbsp mayonnaise over chicken breast.
3. Place pistachios on each piece of chicken breast.
4. Divide the chicken breast mixture into two baskets.
5. Select the "air fry" mode for Zone 1 with 187 degrees C temperature and 15-18 minutes of cooking time.
6. Press the "MATCH COOK" button to copy the setting for Zone 2.
7. Initiate cooking by pressing the "START/PAUSE" button.
8. When done, remove and serve!

Nutrition:

CALORIES: 332KCAL | FAT: 31G | CARBOHYDRATE: 9G | PROTEIN: 58G | FIBER 3G

CHICKEN STREET TACOS

 **PREPARATION TIME** 5 MINUTES

 **COOKING TIME** 10 MINUTES

 **SERVINGS** 4 PERSONS

Ingredients:

- Olive oil, 14ml
- Chicken breast, 1lb, cut into strips
- Chili powder, 10g
- Salt, 5g
- Black pepper, 2g
- Flour tortillas, 12

Optional toppings:
- Onion
- Lettuce
- Tomatoes
- Cheese
- Sour cream

Preparations:

1. Add chicken pieces, pepper, salt, and chili powder into the bowl. Coat it well.
2. Divide mixture into two baskets.
3. Select the "air fry" mode for Zone 1 with 193 degrees C temperature and 10 minutes of cooking time.
4. Press the "MATCH COOK" button to copy the setting for Zone 2.
5. Initiate cooking by pressing the "START/PAUSE" button.
6. When done, serve over street taco tortillas and top with onion, sour cream, cheese, tomatoes, and lettuce.

Nutrition:

CALORIES: 362KCAL | FAT: 11G | CARBOHYDRATE: 34G | PROTEIN: 30G | FIBER 2G

CHICKEN ENCHILADAS

 **PREPARATION TIME** 10 MINUTES   **COOKING TIME** 15 MINUTES   **SERVINGS** 12 PERSONS

Ingredients:

- Flour Tortillas, 20
- Rotisserie Chicken, 1 pound
- Sweet Onion, 1 chopped
- Enchilada Sauce, 828ml, mild
- Brown Sugar, 32g
- Cheese, 1 packet, shredded
- Green Onions, chopped

Preparations:

1. Shred the meat and place it into the bowl. Then, chop the onion.
2. Add enchilada sauce into the saucepan and heat over medium-high flame. Add brown sugar and heat it well. Bring to a boil. Turn off the flame.
3. Place a tortilla onto the plate. Add sauce, onion, chicken, and cheese over it. Fold the tortilla and keep it aside. Place it into the basket.
4. Select the "air fry" mode for Zone 1 with 176 degrees C temperature and 15 minutes of cooking time.
5. Press the "MATCH COOK" button to copy the setting for Zone 2.
6. Initiate cooking by pressing the "START/PAUSE" button.
7. When done, top with black olives, green onion, and sour cream.

Nutrition:

CALORIES: 252KCAL | FAT: 7G | CARBOHYDRATE: 28G | PROTEIN: 18G | FIBER 1G

CHICKEN ENCHILADAS | 63

VEGETABLES

CRUNCHY VEGGIE CHIPS

 **PREPARATION TIME**
5 MINUTES

 COOKING TIME
10 MINUTES

 SERVINGS
2 PERSONS

Ingredients:

- Zucchini, ½
- Sweet potato, ½
- Beet, 1
- Extra-virgin olive oil, 5ml
- Salt, 1g
- Ground black pepper, to taste
- Ranch seasoning, 10g

Preparations:

1. Firstly, thinly slice the beet, sweet potato, and zucchini into rounds with a mandolin or knife.
2. Add veggies slices into the bowl and drizzle with olive oil, and season with pepper and salt. Toss to combine.
3. Divide veggies slices into two baskets.
4. Select the "air fry" mode for Zone 1 with 182 degrees C temperature and 15 minutes of cooking time.
5. Press the "MATCH COOK" button to copy the setting for Zone 2.
6. Initiate cooking by pressing the "START/PAUSE" button.
7. When done, remove chips from the Ninja foodi air fryer.
8. Sprinkle with ranch and serve!

Nutrition:

CALORIES: 79KCAL | FAT: 0.9G | CARBOHYDRATE: 16.6G | SUGAR: 6G | FIBER: 3.4G | PROTEIN: 2.7G

PARMESAN DILL FRIED PICKLE CHIPS

 **PREPARATION TIME** 15 MINUTES

 **COOKING TIME** 16 MINUTES

 **SERVINGS** 4 PERSONS

Ingredients:

- Dill pickles, 907g
- Eggs, 2
- Panko breadcrumbs, 85g
- Parmesan cheese, 43g, grated
- Dried dill weed, 1g, dried

Preparations:

1. Slice the pickles into thick slices and place them among layers of paper towel and pat dry it.
2. Add eggs into the bowl and beat it well.
3. Add dill weed, parmesan cheese, and panko bread crumbs into the re-sealable bag and combine it well.
4. Immerse each pickle slice into the egg mixture and then toss in the panko mixture.
5. Divide coated pickle chips into two baskets.
6. Select the "bake" mode for Zone 1 with 175 degrees C temperature and 8-10 minutes of cooking time.
7. Press the "MATCH COOK" button to copy the setting for Zone 2.
8. Initiate cooking by pressing the "START/PAUSE" button.
9. When done, remove chips from the Ninja foodi air fryer.

Nutrition:

CALORIES: 143KCAL | FAT: 6G | CARBOHYDRATE: 15G | SUGAR: 2G | FIBER: 1G | PROTEIN: 8G

CARROT FRIES

 **PREPARATION TIME** 10 MINUTES

 **COOKING TIME** 15 MINUTES

 **SERVINGS** 4 PERSONS

Ingredients:

- Carrots, 1lb, peeled
- Olive oil, 10ml
- Garlic salt, 2g

Preparations:

1. Slice carrots lengthwise into fries.
2. Add garlic salt and oil into the bowl and toss with carrot fries.
3. Divide fries into two baskets.
4. Select the "bake" mode for Zone 1 with 200 degrees C temperature and 5-10 minutes of cooking time.
5. Press the "MATCH COOK" button to copy the setting for Zone 2.
6. Initiate cooking by pressing the "START/PAUSE" button.
7. When done, remove fries from the Ninja foodi air fryer.
8. Serve and enjoy!

Nutrition:

CALORIES: 60KCAL | FAT: 2G | CARBOHYDRATE: 9G | SUGAR: 4G | FIBER: 3G | PROTEIN: 1G

BUFFALO CAULIFLOWER TOTS

 **PREPARATION TIME**
10 MINUTES

 **COOKING TIME**
20 MINUTES

 **SERVINGS**
6 PERSONS

Ingredients:

- Cauliflower florets, 512g, steamed
- Egg, 1, beaten
- Cheddar cheese, 128g, shredded
- Parmesan cheese, 128g, grated
- Panko breadcrumbs, 85g
- Fresh chives or parsley, 28g
- Salt and pepper, to taste

Preparations:

1. Firstly, steam the cauliflower florets in hot water for three to four minutes. Then, drain it. Transfer it to the food processor and process until you get rice consistency.
2. Squeeze out excess water from the cauliflower with a paper towel.
3. Mix the ingredients into the bowl and season with pepper and salt.
4. Shape mixture into tater-tot shape.
5. Divide it into two baskets.
6. Select the "air fry" mode for Zone 1 with 200 degrees C temperature and 10-12 minutes of cooking time.
7. Press the "MATCH COOK" button to copy the setting for Zone 2.
8. Initiate cooking by pressing the "START/PAUSE" button.
9. When done, remove tots from the Ninja foodi air fryer.
10. When done, serve with tomato ketchup.

Nutrition:

CALORIES: 295KCAL | FAT: 1.7G | CARBOHYDRATE: 16.4G | SUGAR: 2.4G | FIBER: 2.9G | PROTEIN: 20.3G

BEET CHIPS

 **PREPARATION TIME** 15 MINUTES

 **COOKING TIME** 30 MINUTES

 **SERVINGS** 4 PERSONS

Ingredients:

- Beet, 1 ½ lbs, cut into thick slices
- Rapeseed oil, 10ml
- Salt, 1g
- Black pepper, 1g

Preparations:

1. Add pepper, salt, oil, and sliced beets into the big bowl. Toss to combine.
2. Divide it into two baskets.
3. Select the "air fry" mode for Zone 1 with 160 degrees C temperature and 25-30 minutes of cooking time.
4. Press the "MATCH COOK" button to copy the setting for Zone 2.
5. Initiate cooking by pressing the "START/PAUSE" button.
6. When done, remove tots from the Ninja foodi air fryer.
7. Serve and enjoy!

Nutrition:

CALORIES: 47KCAL | FAT: 2G | CARBOHYDRATE: 6G | SUGAR: 4G | FIBER: 2G | PROTEIN: 1G

SPECIAL AVOCADO FRIES

 **PREPARATION TIME** 5 MINUTES

 **COOKING TIME** 10 MINUTES

 **SERVINGS** 4 PERSONS

Ingredients:
- Flour, 64g
- Black pepper, 7g
- Eggs, 2
- Water, 14ml
- Panko breadcrumbs, 64g
- Avocado, 2, cut into 8 wedges
- Salt, 1g
- No-salt-added ketchup, 59ml
- Mayonnaise, 29ml
- Apple cider vinegar, 14ml
- Sriracha chili sauce, 14ml

Preparations:

1. Add pepper and flour into the shallow dish and stir well.
2. Add water and eggs to another dish and beat it.
3. Add panko to 3rd dish—immerse avocado wedges in flour. Dip in egg mixture. Dredge in panko—coat avocado wedges with cooking spray.
4. Divide the avocado wedges into two air fryer baskets.
5. Select the "air fry" mode for Zone 1 with 200 degrees C temperature and 7-8 minutes of cooking time.
6. Press the "MATCH COOK" button to copy the setting for Zone 2.
7. Initiate cooking by pressing the "START/PAUSE" button.
8. When done, remove fries from the Ninja foodi air fryer.
9. Season with salt.
10. Whisk the Sriracha, vinegar, mayonnaise, and ketchup into the bowl.
11. Place avocado fried onto the plate and top with sauce.

Nutrition:

CALORIES: 262KCAL | FAT: 18G | CARBOHYDRATE: 23G | SUGAR: 5G | FIBER: 7G | PROTEIN: 5G

FRIED MUSHROOMS

 **PREPARATION TIME** 10 MINUTES

 **COOKING TIME** 10 MINUTES

 **SERVINGS** 4 PERSONS

Ingredients:

- Oyster mushrooms, 170g, rinsed and dried, broken into large pieces
- Almond milk, 59ml
- Yellow mustard, 14g
- Hot sauce, 5ml
- Flour, 64g
- Seasoned salt, 5g
- Garlic powder, 5g
- Onion powder, 5g
- Italian seasoning, 5g
- Cayenne pepper, 2g

Preparations:

1. Whisk the hot sauce, mustard, and almond milk into the shallow bowl. Keep it aside.
2. Whisk the cayenne pepper, Italian seasoning, onion powder, garlic powder, seasoned flour, and all-purpose flour into the bowl.
3. Coat each mushroom piece in the milk mixture and then coat in the flour mixture. Place coated pieces onto the plate. Put it into the refrigerator for 20 minutes.
4. Divide the avocado wedges into two air fryer baskets.
5. Select the "air fry" mode for Zone 1 with 200 degrees C temperature and 10-12 minutes of cooking time.
6. Press the "MATCH COOK" button to copy the setting for Zone 2.
7. Initiate cooking by pressing the "START/PAUSE" button.
8. When done, remove fried mushrooms from the Ninja foodi air fryer.
9. Serve!

Nutrition:

CALORIES: 91KCAL | FAT: 2G | CARBOHYDRATE: 16G | SUGAR: 1G | FIBER: 2G | PROTEIN: 4G

COURGETTE FRITTERS

 **PREPARATION TIME** 12 MINUTES

 **COOKING TIME** 12 MINUTES

 **SERVINGS** 4 PERSONS

Ingredients:
- Courgette, 2
- Salt, 14g
- Egg, 1
- Flour, 42g
- Garlic powder, 5g
- Onion powder, 1g
- Paprika, 1g
- Black pepper, 1g

Herb Dip:
- Greek Yogurt or Sour Cream, 59ml
- Fresh herbs, 28g
- Garlic, 10g, minced
- Lemon juice, 5ml
- Salt, to taste

Preparations:

1. Rinse, dry, and cut off the ends of zucchini. Grate the zucchini using a box grater.
2. Sprinkle one tbsp salt over grated zucchini. Let rest for 10 minutes.
3. Mix the chopped herbs, salt, lemon juice, and Greek yogurt or sour cream into the bowl. Keep it aside.
4. After ten minutes, squeeze excess water of Courgette with a paper towel and pat it dry. Then, add it to the clean bowl.
5. Add black pepper, paprika, onion powder, garlic powder, egg, and all-purpose flour to the zucchini and stir well.
6. Divide the zucchini mixture into the two baskets.
7. Select the "air fry" mode for Zone 1 with 180 degrees C temperature and 10-12 minutes of cooking time.
8. Press the "MATCH COOK" button to copy the setting for Zone 2.
9. Initiate cooking by pressing the "START/PAUSE" button.
10. When done, remove zucchini fritters from the Ninja foodi air fryer.
11. Top with herb dip.

Nutrition:

CALORIES: 57KCAL | FAT: 1G | CARBOHYDRATE: 8G | SUGAR: 3G | FIBER: 1G | PROTEIN: 3G

TASTY VEGGIE QUESADILLAS

 **PREPARATION TIME** 10 MINUTES

 COOKING TIME 20 MINUTES

 SERVINGS 4 PERSONS

Ingredients:

- Whole-grain flour tortillas, 4
- Cheese, 128g, shredded, low-fat
- Red bell pepper, 128g, sliced
- Zucchini, 128g, sliced
- Black beans, 128g, drained and rinsed
- Greek yogurt, 59ml, low-fat
- 5ml lime zest plus 14ml fresh juice
- Ground cumin, 1g
- Fresh coriander, 28g, chopped
- Pico de gallo, 64g, drained

Preparations:

1. Place tortillas onto the clean work surface.
2. Top with two tbsp shredded cheese over half of each tortilla.
3. Top with black beans, zucchini slices, and red pepper slices, and top with half a cup of cheese. Then, fold over half-moon-shaped quesadillas.
4. Let coat with cooking spray.
5. Divide the quesadillas into two baskets.
6. Select the "air fry" mode for Zone 1 with 200 degrees C temperature and 10 minutes of cooking time.
7. Press the "MATCH COOK" button to copy the setting for Zone 2.
8. Initiate cooking by pressing the "START/PAUSE" button.
9. When done, remove veggie quesadillas from the Ninja foodi air fryer.
10. Meanwhile, add cumin, lime juice, lime zest, and yogurt into the bowl.
11. Cut quesadilla into wedges and garnish with coriander.
12. Serve with cumin cream and pico de gallo.

Nutrition:

CALORIES: 291KCAL | FAT: 8G | CARBOHYDRATE: 36G | SUGAR: 3G | FIBER: 8G | PROTEIN: 17G

KALE CHIPS

 **PREPARATION TIME** 10 MINUTES
 **COOKING TIME** 28 MINUTES
 **SERVINGS** 2 PERSONS

Ingredients:

- Kale leaves, 768g, stems and ribs removed
- Olive oil, 14ml
- Soy sauce, 5ml, low-sodium
- White or black sesame seeds, 5g
- Garlic, 2 ½ g, minced, dried
- Poppy seeds, 1g

Preparations:

1. Rinse and dry kale leaves and then tear them into pieces.
2. Add soy sauce, olive oil, and kale into the bowl and toss to combine.
3. Divide tossed kale into two baskets.
4. Select the "air fry" mode for Zone 1 with 190 degrees C temperature and 28 minutes of cooking time.
5. Press the "MATCH COOK" button to copy the setting for Zone 2.
6. Initiate cooking by pressing the "START/PAUSE" button.
7. Open the lid, sprinkle with poppy seeds, garlic, and sesame seeds and close the lid.
8. When done, remove kale chips from the Ninja foodi air fryer.
9. Serve and enjoy!

Nutrition:

CALORIES: 159KCAL | FAT: 8G | CARBOHYDRATE: 20G | SUGAR: 0G | FIBER: 5G | PROTEIN: 7G

KALE CHIPS | 75

SNACKS AND DESSERTS

CHOCOLATE CHIP COOKIES

 PREPARATION TIME 10 MINUTES
 COOKING TIME 5 MINUTES
 SERVINGS 18 PERSONS

Ingredients:

- Unsalted butter, 118ml
- Brown sugar, 64g
- White sugar, 32g
- Egg, 1
- Vanilla extract, 5ml
- Flour, 192g
- Bicarb soda, 5g
- Salt, 1g
- Semi-sweet chocolate chips, 128g

Preparations:

1. Add butter into the microwave-safe bowl and microwave it for 10 to 20 seconds until melted.
2. Add melted butter, white sugar, and brown sugar and beat it well.
3. Add vanilla and egg and beat it for 30 seconds. Add remaining ingredients and stir well.
4. Put it into the fridge to chill for 30 minutes. Place mixture into the air fryer basket.
5. Place air fryer basket to the Ninja foodi air fryer.
6. Select the "bake" mode for Zone 1 with 162 degrees C temperature and 5-7 minutes of cooking time.
7. Press the "MATCH COOK" button to copy the setting for Zone 2.
8. Initiate cooking by pressing the "START/PAUSE" button.
9. When done, remove cookies from the Ninja foodi air fryer.
10. Serve and enjoy!

Nutrition:

CALORIES: 179KCAL | FAT: 9G | CARBOHYDRATE: 22G | SUGAR: 12G | FIBER: 1G | PROTEIN: 2G

BLUEBERRY MUFFINS

 **PREPARATION TIME** 15 MINUTES  **COOKING TIME** 17 MINUTES  **SERVINGS** 3 PERSONS

Ingredients:

- Egg, 1
- Sugar, 65g
- Oil, 80ml
- Water, 30ml
- Vanilla extract, 1 ml
- Lemon zest, 5ml
- Flour, 80g
- Baking powder, 2 ½ g
- Blueberries, 75g

Preparations:

1. Combine wet ingredients into a bowl and keep it aside.
2. Whisk dry ingredients in a small bowl. Then, add dry ingredients to the wet ingredients. Place mixture into the muffin tins.
3. Divide the muffin tins into two baskets.
4. Place air fryer basket to the Ninja foodi air fryer.
5. Select the "air fry" mode for Zone 1 with 175 degrees C temperature and 15-17 minutes of cooking time.
6. Press the "MATCH COOK" button to copy the setting for Zone 2.
7. Initiate cooking by pressing the "START/PAUSE" button.
8. When done, remove muffin tins from the Ninja foodi air fryer.
9. When done, remove and serve!

Nutrition:

CALORIES: 39KCAL | FAT: 3G | CARBOHYDRATE: 1G | SUGAR: 1G | FIBER: 0G | PROTEIN: 2G

PECAN PIE

 **PREPARATION TIME** 5 MINUTES

 **COOKING TIME** 30 MINUTES

 **SERVINGS** 8 PERSONS

Ingredients:

- Light corn syrup, 236ml
- Brown sugar, 128g
- Butter, 78ml, melted
- Vanilla, 10ml
- Salt, 2g
- Eggs, 3
- Pecans, 192g, chopped
- Pie crust, 1

Preparations:

1. Firstly, bake the pie crust at 160 degrees C for three to four minutes into the 2 baskets Ninja air fryer. When done, remove it.
2. Add salt, vanilla, melted butter, brown sugar, and corn syrup into the bowl and combine it well.
3. Whisk eggs into the bowl. Add pecans and then add to the egg mixture. When combined, place the mixture into the pie crust.
4. Place it into the air fryer basket.
5. Select the "air fry" mode for Zone 1 with 176 degrees C temperature and 30-35 minutes of cooking time.
6. Press the "MATCH COOK" button to copy the setting for Zone 2.
7. Initiate cooking by pressing the "START/PAUSE" button.
8. When done, remove pie crust from the Ninja foodi air fryer.
9. When done, remove and serve!

Nutrition:

CALORIES: 499KCAL | FAT: 22G | CARBOHYDRATE: 74G | SUGAR: 61G | FIBER: 2G | PROTEIN: 6G

RED VELVET CAKE MIX COOKIES

 **PREPARATION TIME**
5 MINUTES

 COOKING TIME
10 MINUTES

 SERVINGS
12 PERSONS

Ingredients:

- Red velvet cake mix, 1 packet
- Eggs, 2
- Vegetable oil, 118ml
- White chocolate chips, 96g

Preparations:

1. Firstly, place parchment paper into an air fryer basket.
2. Poke holes in the paper.
3. Meanwhile, mix eggs, oil, and cake mix into the mixing bowl. Make the thick dough.
4. Add white chocolate chips and combine them into the cookie dough.
5. Divide dough into two baskets. OR. Place the dough into the basket.
6. Select the "air fry" mode for Zone 1 with 187 degrees C temperature and 4-5 minutes of cooking time.
7. Press the "MATCH COOK" button to copy the setting for Zone 2.
8. Initiate cooking by pressing the "START/PAUSE" button.
9. When done, remove cookies from the Ninja foodi air fryer.
10. Serve and enjoy!

Nutrition:

CALORIES: 305KCAL | FAT: 2G | CARBOHYDRATE: 33G | SUGAR: 20G | FIBER: 1G | PROTEIN: 4G

CHERRY PIE BOMBS

 **PREPARATION TIME** 5 MINUTES

 COOKING TIME 10 MINUTES

 SERVINGS 4 PERSONS

Ingredients:

- Cherry pie filling, 595g
- Biscuits, 453g, big-sized
- Cinnamon, 5g
- Granulated white sugar, 42g

Preparations:

1. Add sugar and cinnamon into the bowl. Keep it aside.
2. Peel each biscuit into two layers. Roll each layer into a circle.
3. Place cherry pie filling into the middle of each circle.
4. Pinch to seal and roll them into the balls.
5. Divide bombs into two baskets. OR. Place pie cherry bombs into the basket.
6. Select the "air fry" mode for Zone 1 with 176 degrees C temperature and 8-9 minutes of cooking time.
7. Press the "MATCH COOK" button to copy the setting for Zone 2.
8. Initiate cooking by pressing the "START/PAUSE" button.
9. When done, remove pie cherry bombs from the Ninja foodi air fryer.
10. Then, roll in the sugar and cinnamon mixture.
11. Serve and enjoy!

Nutrition:

CALORIES: 629KCAL | FAT: 19G | CARBOHYDRATE: 107G | SUGAR: 13G | FIBER: 3G | PROTEIN: 8G

CONCLUSION

You have completed your first step to culinary freedom. You can now cook in an unheated kitchen.

The next step from here is to explore even further and find your own culinary footing! Learn the basics from this recipes, and come up with your very own awesome Ninja Foodi Friendly recipes and make your ultimate meal plan!

The Ninja Foodi possesses the unique ability to micro-wave food, so if you are looking for a one-stop-shop for your food-cooking needs, it really doesn't get any better than the Ninja Foodi! You see, with just one appliance, you will be able to make the staples of your diet! You will be able to make rice, soup, stews, pastas, deep fried foods, and vegetable dishes, all with the simple touch of a button! So, what you are telling yourself at. This is far too good to be true! I know, I know! Of course, the question on your mind would definitely be: how can the Ninja Foodi deliver such great attributes for such a low price? Instead of having to spend over a hundred dollars on a rice cooker, a slow cooker, and an air fryer, the Ninja Foodi has all of those functions in one tiny, inexpensive appliance. Not only does it have those attributes, but it is able to take your cooking to the next level. Now, you can make the most delicious steamed or deep fried foods in your own home! Your whole family will be motivated to eat clean and more often, all because you singlehandedly took control of your kitchen! Lastly, if you feel like your Ninja Foodi is just not up to snuff, don't worry! Ninja Foodi is not like any other appliance that you will probably ever encounter. A Ninja Foodist always trusts and follows their instincts, and you should too. The Ninja Foodist rewards us for doing so. Ninja Foodist that is what we ninja's are training to become. If you look at the Ninja Foodi Cam you'll notice that it is almost the same size as the Ninja Foodi itself, but for ninja training purposes we must use the Cam to train our reflexes. Just like one must when learning to use a silent but deadly weapon like the Shurikon. A Ninja Foodist learns to be able to respond to any situation in a relatively quick manner, and when training like this, we must do so much faster than ever before. Like Ninja Foodist's already do, we must do so while dealing with a situation on a much larger scale.

Fire is still a big deal, so keep on practicing ... please. Try to avoid meat or fish in most of your meals, or you'll get massive heartburn. Enjoy your Ninja Cooking skills! It is fun to create new recipes and experiment. You don't need a microwave, just add foil, aluminum foil, etc to your dishes to be heated. Making beans in your Ninja Cooking is great. Since they are very water soluble, they will add their own water to your dish when you cook them. Plates, bowls, baking sheets and glass will work just as well as induction cooktops or a non-microwave oven.

You are now a culinary ninja. Enjoy cooking your favorite Ninja Foodi Friendly meals and recipes!

INDEX

B
BARBEQUE CHICKEN SAUSAGE PIZZA............57
BBQ PORK TENDERLOIN WITH MUSHROOMS......49
BEEF AND BROCCOLI............................39
BEEF, LAMB AND PORK..........................28
BEEF MEATLOAF.................................30
BEEF ROAST AND POTATO FRIES 42
BEEF WITH RATATOUILLE.........................45
BEET CHIPS....................................69
BLACK COD WITH BLACK BEAN SAUCE............24
BLUEBERRY MUFFINS............................78
BREAKFAST ONION OMELET......................12
BREAKFAST RECIPES 10
BROWN SUGAR AND HONEY GLAZED HAM........33
BUFFALO CAULIFLOWER TOTS....................68
BUFFALO CHICKEN CALZONES....................58
BURGERS......................................43

C
CAJUN SEASONED FRIED CATFISH...............26
CARROT FRIES.................................67
CHERRY PIE BOMBS.............................81
CHICKEN BURGER...............................56
CHICKEN ENCHILADAS..........................62
CHICKEN LEG QUARTERS.........................55
CHICKEN STREET TACOS.........................61
CHOCOLATE CHIP COOKIES......................77
COCONUT SHRIMP WITH DIPPING SAUCE.........19
COD NUGGETS..................................23
COURGETTE FRITTERS...........................72

CRUNCHY VEGGIE CHIPS........................65

D
DELICIOUS CHICKEN MEATBALLS.................59
DELICIOUS PUMPKIN BREAD......................15

E
EGG AND BACON MUFFINS.......................11
EGG SALAD SANDWICHES........................14

F
FISH AND SEAFOOD.............................16
FRIED MUSHROOMS.............................71

G
GARLIC LAMB CHOPS POTATO WEDGES..........46
GREEK LAMB BURGERS..........................36

I
INDEX...83

J
JUMBO SHRIMP.................................20

K
KALE CHIPS....................................74

L
LAMB MEATBALLS...............................37
LAMB SHANKS WITH BUTTERNUT SQUASH FRIES..47

M
MEAL PLAN....................................85
MUSHROOM AND SQUASH TOAST.................13
MUSSELS.......................................22

P
PARMESAN DILL FRIED PICKLE CHIPS.............66
PECAN PIE.....................................79

INDEX | 83

PISTACHIO CRUSTED CHICKEN	60
POPCORN CHICKEN	54
PORK CHOP BITES WITH MUSHROOMS	31
PORK CHOPS PARMIGIANA	34
PORK LETTUCE WRAPS	29
PORK LOIN SANDWICH WITH GREEN TOMATOES	50
PORK SCHNITZEL	38
PORK SCHNITZEL AND POTATO HAY	51
POULTRY	52
PRAWNS	21

R

RED VELVET CAKE MIX COOKIES	80
ROAST LAMB	35
SALMON CAKES	17

S

SNACKS AND DESSERTS	76
SPECIAL AVOCADO FRIES	70
STEAK BITES WITH GARLIC BUTTER	40
STEAK BITES WITH MUSHROOMS	41
STUFFED ZUCCHINI BOATS WITH SAUSAGE	32
SWAI FISH	18

T

TAQUITOS WITH GREEN BEANS	44
TASTY VEGGIE QUESADILLAS	73
TONKATSU WITH WHITE RICE	48
TUNA STEAKS	25

V

VEGETABLES	64

Y

YUMMY CHICKEN CUTLETS	53

MEAL PLAN

DAY: 1		
BREAKFAST	**LUNCH**	**DINNER**
Banana nut oatmeal cup and one Clementine	Veggie and hummus sandwich	Chicken Fajita bowl with brown rice
Calories 387kcal	Calories 325kcal	Calories 507kcal

DAY: 2		
BREAKFAST	**LUNCH**	**DINNER**
Banana nut cereal	Cauliflower taco bowls	Courgette chickpea veggie burger with tahini ranch sauce and sweet potato fries
Calories 220kcal	Calories 344kcal	Calories 495kcal

DAY: 3		
BREAKFAST	**LUNCH**	**DINNER**
Banana Bread	BBQ beef stir fry	Fish stew
Calories 186kcal	Calories 310kcal	Calories 389kcal

DAY: 4		
BREAKFAST	**LUNCH**	**DINNER**
Breakfast frittata	Peachy pork with rice	Pumpkin waffles
Calories 147kcal	Calories 387kcal	Calories 183kcal

DAY: 5		
BREAKFAST	**LUNCH**	**DINNER**
French toast sticks	Fish sticks	Chicken burgers
Calories 206kcal	Calories 325kcal	Calories 281kcal

DAY: 6		
BREAKFAST	**LUNCH**	**DINNER**
Poached egg caprese	Cucumber egg salad	Ground beef and bar-ley bowls
Calories 482kcal	Calories 176kcal	Calories 238kcal

DAY: 7		
BREAKFAST	**LUNCH**	**DINNER**
Feta and spinach frittata	courgette quiche	Lamb chops
Calories 152kcal	Calories 145kcal	Calories 465kcal

Printed in Great Britain
by Amazon